Bernie Sanders.
The Little Black Book

"May the wisdom of the greatest minds become yours."
S. C. Hollister

Red Pocket Book Publishing

Bernie Sanders. The Little Black Book

Design Copyright © 2015 S.C. Hollister
Published by Red Pocket Book Publishing
PO Box 14204
SLO, CA 93406-4204

To Bernie Sanders,
Thank you.

BERNIE SANDERS

CONTENTS

The Little Black Book used to be a means of getting in touch with people who could give you what you wanted; most famously understood as a Booty Call book.

But, in this 21st century version of the little black book, wisdom and knowledge are the keys to opening doors.

The design of this book invites you to meditate on the wisdom within, have focused conversations, or protect your coffee table from condensation.

The Bernie Sanders Little Black Book starts with general quotes from Sanders. After that, major campaign issues are in alphabetical order. They are all equally important.

May the wisdom of some of the greatest, become yours.

Bernie Sanders

Bernie Sanders.

The Little Black Book

Bernie Sanders

Bernie's Little Black Book

~

1. I am going to do my best to try to create a country in which children are not living in poverty, in which kids can go to college, in which old people have health care. Will I succeed? I can't guarantee you that, but I can tell you that from a human point of view, it is better to show up than to give up.

2. Don't underestimate me.

3. When we stand together, we will always win. When men and women stand together for justice, we win. When black, white and Hispanic people stand together for

JUSTICE, WE WIN. WHEN STRAIGHT AND GAY PEOPLE STAND TOGETHER FOR JUSTICE, WE WIN. WHEN YOUNG AND OLD STAND TOGETHER FOR JUSTICE, WE WIN. WHEN WORKING FAMILIES STAND TOGETHER, WE WIN.

4. THERE IS A LOT OF SENTIMENT THAT ENOUGH IS ENOUGH, THAT WE NEED FUNDAMENTAL CHANGES, THAT THE ESTABLISHMENT – WHETHER IT IS THE ECONOMIC ESTABLISHMENT, THE POLITICAL ESTABLISHMENT, OR THE MEDIA ESTABLISHMENT – IS FAILING THE AMERICAN PEOPLE.

5. THEY HAVE THE MONEY, BUT WE'VE GOT THE PEOPLE.

6. THE TIME HAS COME WHEN THE OLD WORLD MUST MAKE WAY FOR THE NEW.

7. DIFFICULT TIMES OFTEN BRING OUT THE BEST IN PEOPLE.

8. WE ARE LIVING IN A NATION AND IN A WORLD WHICH WORSHIPS NOT LOVE OF BROTHERS AND SISTERS, NOT LOVE OF THE POOR AND THE SICK, BUT WORSHIPS THE ACQUISITION OF MONEY AND GREAT WEALTH. I DON'T THINK THAT IS THE COUNTRY WE SHOULD BE LIVING IN.

9. WE ARE LIVING IN THE RICHEST COUNTRY IN THE HISTORY OF THE WORLD, YET WE HAVE THE HIGHEST RATE OF CHILDHOOD POVERTY OF ALMOST ANY MAJOR COUNTRY AND MILLIONS OF PEOPLE ARE STRUGGLING TO PUT FOOD ON THE TABLE. IT IS MY ABSOLUTE CONVICTION THAT EVERYONE IN THIS COUNTRY DESERVES A MINIMUM STANDARD

OF LIVING AND WE'VE GOT TO GO FORWARD IN THE FIGHT TO MAKE THAT HAPPEN.

10. THE U.S. CURRENTLY SPENDS MORE MONEY ON THE MILITARY THAN THE NEXT NINE COUNTRIES COMBINED. YET, DESPITE SOME 45 MILLION AMERICANS LIVING IN POVERTY, 35 MILLION WITHOUT HEALTH CARE AND VETERANS THROUGHOUT THE COUNTRY SLEEPING OUT ON THE STREETS, THE ONLY PROGRAM THAT REPUBLICANS WANT TO INCREASE FUNDING FOR IS THE MILITARY. WHY?

11. OVERALL, WE NEED BOLD CHANGE IN OUR CRIMINAL JUSTICE SYSTEM. A GOOD FIRST STEP FORWARD IS TO START TREATING PRISONERS AS HUMAN BEINGS, NOT PROFITING FROM THEIR INCARCERATION.

Our emphasis must be on rehabilitation, not incarceration and longer prison sentences.

12. If you want to defend the middle class you don't cut Social Security, you don't cut Medicare, and you don't cut benefits for disabled vets.

13. When a wife is diagnosed with cancer and a husband cannot get time off of work to take care of her, that is not a family value. That is an attack on everything that a family is supposed to stand for.

14. I believe in a society where all people do well, not just a handful of billionaires.

NOTES

CLIMATE CHANGE

15. I believe, along with Pope Francis and almost all scientists, that climate change is threatening this planet in horrendous ways, and that we have to be aggressive in transforming our energy system away from fossil fuel and defeat the Keystone Pipeline.

16. Right now, we have an energy policy that is rigged to boost the profits of big oil companies like Exxon, BP, and Shell at the expense of average Americans. CEO's are raking in record profits while climate change ravages our planet and our people – all because the wealthiest industry in the history of

OUR PLANET HAS BRIBED POLITICIANS INTO COMPLACENCY IN THE FACE OF CLIMATE CHANGE. ENOUGH IS ENOUGH.

17. CLIMATE CHANGE IS REAL, CAUSED BY HUMAN ACTIVITY AND ALREADY DEVASTATING OUR NATION AND PLANET. THE UNITED STATES MUST LEAD THE WORLD IN COMBATING CLIMATE CHANGE AND TRANSFORMING OUR ENERGY SYSTEM AWAY FROM FOSSIL FUELS AND TOWARD ENERGY EFFICIENCY AND SUSTAINABILITY.

18. SUBSIDIES FOR THE OIL, GAS AND COAL INDUSTRIES ARE PROJECTED TO COST TAXPAYERS MORE THAN $135 BILLION IN THE COMING DECADE. AT A TIME WHEN SCIENTISTS TELL US WE NEED TO REDUCE CARBON POLLUTION TO PREVENT CATASTROPHIC CLIMATE

CHANGE, IT IS ABSURD TO PROVIDE MASSIVE SUBSIDIES THAT PAD FOSSIL-FUEL COMPANIES' ALREADY ENORMOUS PROFITS.

19. AS THE NATION AT LAST CONFRONTS GLOBAL WARMING, IT IS NO TIME FOR DENIAL, GREED, CYNICISM OR PESSIMISM.

20. WHEN WE REJECT SCIENCE, WE BECOME THE LAUGHINGSTOCK OF THE WORLD.

21. AT A TIME WHEN OUR PLANET IS WARMING DUE TO CLIMATE CHANGE, THE LAST THING OUR ENVIRONMENT NEEDS IS MORE DRILLING. WHAT WE NEED IS FOR CONGRESS AND THE WHITE HOUSE TO MOVE TOWARD CLEAN ENERGY SUCH AS SOLAR, WIND AND GEOTHERMAL.

Notes

CORPORATE AMERICA

22. BEN IS A PERSON; JERRY IS A PERSON; BEN AND JERRY'S IS NOT A PERSON.

23. LET US WAGE A MORAL AND POLITICAL WAR AGAINST THE BILLIONAIRES AND CORPORATE LEADERS, ON WALL STREET AND ELSEWHERE, WHOSE POLICIES AND GREED ARE DESTROYING THE MIDDLE CLASS OF AMERICA.

24. IT IS MORALLY REPUGNANT AND A NATIONAL TRAGEDY THAT WE HAVE PRIVATIZED PRISONS ALL OVER AMERICA. IN MY VIEW, CORPORATIONS SHOULD NOT BE ALLOWED TO MAKE A PROFIT BY BUILDING MORE JAILS AND KEEPING MORE AMERICANS

BEHIND BARS. WE HAVE GOT TO END THE PRIVATE-FOR-PRIVATE RACKET IN AMERICA.

25. IT IS AN OBSCENITY THAT WE STIGMATIZE SO MANY YOUNG AMERICANS WITH A CRIMINAL RECORD FOR SMOKING MARIJUANA, BUT NOT ONE MAJOR WALL STREET EXECUTIVE HAS BEEN PROSECUTED FOR THE NEAR COLLAPSE OF OUR ENTIRE ECONOMY.

26. IN 1983, 50 CORPORATIONS CONTROLLED A MAJORITY OF MEDIA IN AMERICA. IN 1990 THE NUMBER HAD DROPPED TO 23. IN 1997, 10. AND TODAY, SIX... DESPITE THE LACK OF CONVERSATION ON THIS ISSUE OF MEDIA CONCENTRATION, IN PEOPLE'S GUTS, PEOPLE KNOW THAT THIS IS A HUGE ISSUE. THAT

WE CAN'T BE THE DEMOCRACY WE WANT TO BE WHEN SO FEW PEOPLE CONTROL WHAT PEOPLE READ, SEE, AND HEAR.

27. I BELIEVE THAT WHEN A MOTHER GOES TO THE STORE AND PURCHASES FOOD FOR HER CHILD, SHE HAS THE RIGHT TO KNOW WHAT SHE IS FEEDING HER CHILD. IT'S NO MYSTERY WHY MONSANTO WOULD FIGHT PEOPLE'S RIGHT TO KNOW. CLEARLY, THEY HAVE A LOT TO PROTECT.

28. TODAY, VIRTUALLY NO PIECE OF LEGISLATION CAN GET PASSED UNLESS IT HAS THE OKAY FROM CORPORATE AMERICA.

Notes

DISCRIMINATION

29. Sandra Bland, Michael Brown, Rekia Boyd, Eric Garner, Walter Scott, Freddie Gray, Tamir Rice. We know their names. Each of them died unarmed at the hands of police officers or in police custody. The chants are growing louder. People are angry. I am angry. And people have a right to be angry. Violence and brutality of any kind, particularly at the hands of law enforcement sworn to protect and serve our communities, is unacceptable and must not be tolerated.

30. If we stand for anything, we have got to stand together and end all forms of racism,

AND I WILL LEAD THAT EFFORT AS PRESIDENT OF THE UNITED STATES.

31. IT IS MY VERY STRONG VIEW THAT A SOCIETY WHICH PROCLAIMS HUMAN FREEDOM AS ITS GOAL, AS THE UNITED STATES DOES, MUST WORK UNCEASINGLY TO END DISCRIMINATION AGAINST ALL PEOPLE.

32. AMERICANS' RIGHT TO FREE SPEECH SHOULD NOT BE PROPORTIONATE TO THEIR BANK ACCOUNTS.

Notes

DRUGS

33. Addiction is a disease, not a criminal activity.

34. There is no question that the War on Drugs has been a failure.

35. We need to rethink the so-called War on Drugs and take marijuana out of the federal Controlled Substance Act. We need to treat substance abuse as a serious health issue, not a criminal issue. We need to understand that across this country, we have a major crisis in opiate addiction and we need a revolution in mental health treatment so that all people – regardless of their income – can get the help they need.

36. INSTEAD OF REMOVING THE CONDITIONS THAT MAKE PEOPLE DEPRESSED, MODERN SOCIETY GIVES THEM ANTIDEPRESSANT DRUGS. IN EFFECT ANTIDEPRESSANTS ARE A MEANS OF MODIFYING AN INDIVIDUAL'S INTERNAL STATE IN SUCH A WAY AS TO ENABLE HIM TO TOLERATE SOCIAL CONDITIONS THAT HE WOULD OTHERWISE FIND INTOLERABLE.

37. TOO MANY AMERICANS HAVE SEEN THEIR LIVES DESTROYED BECAUSE THEY HAVE CRIMINAL RECORDS AS A RESULT OF MARIJUANA USE. THAT'S WRONG.

38. WE HAVE BEEN ENGAGED IN THE WAR ON DRUGS FOR DECADES NOW WITH A HUGE COST AND THE DESTRUCTION OF A WHOLE LOT OF LIVES OF PEOPLE WHO WERE

NEVER INVOLVED IN ANY VIOLENT ACTIVITIES.

39. ALTHOUGH ABOUT THE SAME PROPORTION OF BLACKS AND WHITES USE MARIJUANA, A BLACK PERSON IS ALMOST FOUR TIMES MORE LIKELY TO BE ARRESTED FOR MARIJUANA POSSESSION THAN A WHITE PERSON.

Notes

EDUCATION

40. QUALITY EDUCATION IN AMERICA, FROM CHILD CARE TO HIGHER EDUCATION MUST BE AFFORDABLE FOR ALL.

41. MANY YOUNG PEOPLE ARE LEAVING SCHOOL DEEPLY IN DEBT FOR WHAT? FOR THE CRIME OF TRYING TO GET AN EDUCATION AND MAKE IT TO THE MIDDLE CLASS.

42. IT MAKES NO SENSE TO ME THAT THE UNITED STATES OF AMERICA HAS MORE JAILS AND PRISONS THAN COLLEGES AND UNIVERSITIES.

43. EDUCATION SHOULD BE A RIGHT, NOT A PRIVILEGE. WE NEED A REVOLUTION IN THE WAY THAT

THE UNITED STATES FUNDS HIGHER EDUCATION.

44. WE ARE MOVING IN EXACTLY THE WRONG DIRECTION IN HIGHER EDUCATION. FORTY YEARS AGO SOME OF OUR GREAT PUBLIC UNIVERSITIES, AS WELL AS MANY STATE COLLEGES, WERE VIRTUALLY TUITION FREE. TODAY, THE COST OF COLLEGE IS UNAFFORDABLE FOR MANY. IN 1990, THE U.S. LED THE WORLD IN THE PERCENTAGES OF 25-34 YEAR OLDS WITH COLLEGE DEGREES. TODAY, WE ARE IN 12TH PLACE. THINGS NEED TO CHANGE. HIGHER EDUCATION MUST BECOME AFFORDABLE FOR ALL.

NOTES

GOVERNMENT REFORM

45. What is interesting about all of this is that we had a very vigorous debate here in the Senate and in the House over the $700 billion TARP program. Every person in America could turn on C-SPAN and hear that debate. They could hear what President Bush had to say, hear what then-Senator Obama and Senator McCain had to say. It was all pretty public. But what took place at the Fed, which, in fact, amounted to a larger bailout, was done behind closed doors. Over three trillion was lent with zero transparency.

46. Democracy should not be a war between one group of billionaire donors and another. That's why we've got to overturn Citizens United and move toward the public funding of elections.

47. In my view, the NSA is out of control and operating in an unconstitutional manner. I worry very much about kids growing up in a society where they think 'I'm not going to talk about this issue, read this book, or explore this idea because someone may think I'm a terrorist.' That is not the kind of free society I want for our children.

48. American democracy is not about billionaires being able to buy candidates and

ELECTIONS. IT IS NOT ABOUT THE KOCH BROTHERS, SHELDON ADELSON AND OTHER INCREDIBLY WEALTHY INDIVIDUALS SPENDING BILLIONS OF DOLLARS TO ELECT CANDIDATES WHO WILL MAKE THE RICH RICHER AND EVERYONE ELSE POORER. ACCORDING TO MEDIA REPORTS THE KOCH BROTHERS ALONE, ONE FAMILY, WILL SPEND MORE MONEY IN THIS ELECTION CYCLE THAN EITHER THE DEMOCRATIC OR REPUBLICAN PARTIES. THIS IS NOT DEMOCRACY. THIS IS OLIGARCHY.

49. NOW IS THE TIME TO ALTER OUR GOVERNMENT. NOW IS THE TIME TO STOP THE MOVEMENT TOWARD OLIGARCHY. NOW IS THE TIME TO CREATE A GOVERNMENT WHICH REPRESENTS ALL AMERICANS AND NOT JUST THE 1%... NO MORE EXCUSES. WE MUST ALL BECOME

INVOLVED IN THE POLITICAL PROCESS.

50. IF THE UNITED STATES SENATE HAD 83 WOMEN AND 17 MEN, RATHER THAN 83 MEN AND 17 WOMEN, MY STRONG GUESS IS THAT A BILL LIKE THIS WOULD NEVER MAKE IT TO THE FLOOR.

51. WE ALL REMEMBER ABRAHAM LINCOLN'S WONDERFUL REMARKS AT GETTYSBURG IN WHICH HE DESCRIBES AMERICA AS A COUNTRY "OF THE PEOPLE, BY THE PEOPLE AND FOR THE PEOPLE." WELL, WITH THE CITIZENS UNITED SUPREME COURT DECISION WE ARE RAPIDLY BECOMING A NATION OF THE VERY RICH, BY THE VERY RICH AND FOR THE VERY RICH. AND THAT IS A HORRENDOUS TRAGEDY. THIS IS NOT THE AMERICA THAT MEN AND

WOMEN THROUGHOUT OUR HISTORY FOUGHT AND DIED TO DEFEND.

52. MILLIONS ARE UNEMPLOYED AND OUR ROADS AND BRIDGES ARE FALLING APART. IF WE CAN SPEND SIX TRILLION DOLLARS SENDING PEOPLE TO WAR, WE CAN SPEND ONE TRILLION DOLLARS TO PUT AMERICANS TO WORK FIXING OUR NATION'S CRUMBLING INFRASTRUCTURE. LET'S REBUILD AMERICA AND CREATE JOBS.

53. WHAT I THINK REALLY HAPPENED IS ABOUT 64% OF THE AMERICAN PEOPLE REJECTED THE 2-PARTY SYSTEM. THEY REJECTED WASHINGTON AS IT NOW FUNCTIONS. THEY REJECTED A POLITICAL SYSTEM AND A CONGRESS THAT SPENDS MORE TIME REPRESENTING THE

wealthy and the powerful than ordinary Americans.

54. We're going to win because first we're going to explain what Democratic socialism is.

55. The Koch brothers' bid to buy elections in America speaks to the obvious need for a constitutional amendment to overturn Citizens United and subsequent rulings. When one wealthy family spends more money than was raised altogether by the last Republican presidential candidate [$400 million], it tells us that we are no longer a country of the people, by the people and for the people. We are becoming a country of the rich, by the rich or for the rich.

56. ARE WE PREPARED TO TAKE ON THE ENORMOUS ECONOMIC AND POLITICAL POWER OF THE BILLIONAIRE CLASS OR DO WE CONTINUE TO SLIDE INTO ECONOMIC AND POLITICAL OLIGARCHY?

57. YOU GO TO SCANDINAVIA, AND YOU WILL FIND THAT PEOPLE HAVE A MUCH HIGHER STANDARD OF LIVING, IN TERMS OF EDUCATION, HEALTH CARE AND DECENT PAYING JOBS.

58. THE RULING HAS RADICALLY CHANGED THE NATURE OF OUR DEMOCRACY. IT HAS FURTHER TILTED THE BALANCE OF THE POWER TOWARD THE RICH AND THE POWERFUL... HISTORY WILL RECORD THAT THE CITIZENS UNITED DECISION IS ONE OF THE

WORST IN THE HISTORY OF OUR COUNTRY.

59. WHEN YOU GO TO YOUR PUBLIC LIBRARY, WHEN YOU CALL YOUR FIRE DEPARTMENT OR THE POLICE DEPARTMENT, WHAT DO YOU THINK YOU'RE CALLING? THESE ARE SOCIALIST INSTITUTIONS.

60. THE AMERICAN PEOPLE ARE SICK AND TIRED OF HEARING ABOUT YOUR DAMN EMAILS.

Notes

GOVERNMENT SPENDING

61. 60% OF THE DISCRETIONARY BUDGET GOES *NOT* TO OUR KIDS, *NOT* TO OUR ELDERLY, *NOT* TO STUDENTS, *NOT* TO WORKING PEOPLE, *NOT* TO INFRASTRUCTURE, *NOT* TO ALL OF THE HUGE UNMET NEEDS WE FACE AS A COUNTRY. IT GOES TO THE MILITARY. THAT'S WHY I VOTED "NO" ON THIS SPENDING BILL.

62. WE'VE CUT BACK ON EDUCATION. WE'VE CUT BACK ON NUTRITION PROGRAMS. WE'VE THROWN KIDS OFF HEAD START. WE HAVE BILLIONS TO SPEND ON WAR BUT NO MONEY TO TAKE CARE OF THE VERY PRESSING NEEDS OF THE AMERICAN PEOPLE. THAT BOTHERS ME A LOT.

63. BALANCING THE BUDGET ON THE BACKS OF THE ELDERLY, THE SICK, THE CHILDREN AND THE POOR IS NOT ONLY IMMORAL, IT IS BAD ECONOMIC POLICY. IT IS SOMETHING THAT MUST BE VIGOROUSLY OPPOSED.

Notes

GUN CONTROL

64. Here is the very sad truth: It is very difficult for the American people to keep up with the mass shootings that we seem to see almost every day. It's time Congress listened to the American people and passed common-sense gun safety legislation.

65. Nobody should have a gun who has a criminal background or who's involved in domestic abuse situations.

Notes

_____

_____

_____

_____

_____

HEALTHCARE

66. HEALTH CARE IS A HUMAN RIGHT, NOT ONLY A RIGHT FOR CORPORATIONS TO PROFIT.

67. AMERICAN'S SHOULD NOT HAVE TO LIVE IN FEAR THAT THEY WILL GO BANKRUPT IF THEY GET SICK.

68. IS IT POSSIBLE TO HAVE A HEALTH CARE SYSTEM IN WHICH DOCTORS AND NURSES HAVE THE TIME TO ADEQUATELY CARE FOR THEIR PATIENTS, RATHER THAN FILL A QUOTA SYSTEM ESTABLISHED BY THE INSURANCE COMPANIES? IS IT POSSIBLE TO HAVE A HEALTH CARE SYSTEM IN WHICH PRESCRIPTION DRUGS ARE AVAILABLE TO PATIENTS BASED ON THEIR NEED, NOT ON THE PROFIT REQUIREMENTS OF THE PHARMACEUTICAL INDUSTRY? I

think so. That's the system we have to fight for.

69. It is incomprehensible that drug companies still get away with charging Americans twice as much, or more, than citizens of Canada or Europe for the exact same drugs manufactured by the exact same companies.

70. Health care must be recognized as a right, not a privilege. Every man, woman and child in our county should be able to access the health care they need regardless of their income. The only long-term solution to America's health care crisis is a single-payer national health care program.

Notes

IMMIGRATION

71. I, MYSELF, AM THE SON OF AN IMMIGRANT. THEIR STORY, MY STORY, OUR STORY, IS A STORY OF AMERICA. IT IS A STORY THAT CONTINUES TO THIS DAY IN FAMILIES ALL ACROSS THE UNITED STATES.

72. I AM A STRONG SUPPORTER OF IMMIGRATION REFORM, AND THE NEED TO PROVIDE A PATHWAY TO CITIZENSHIP FOR 11 MILLION UNDOCUMENTED IMMIGRANTS. I VERY STRONGLY SUPPORT THE DREAM ACT, AND WILL CONTINUE TO STRONGLY SUPPORT IT.

73. DEFERRED ACTION SHOULD INCLUDE THE PARENTS OF CITIZENS, PARENTS OF LEGAL, PERMANENT RESIDENTS AND THE PARENTS OF DREAMERS.

74. It is time to bring our neighbors out of the shadows. It is time to give them legal status. It is time to create a reasonable path to citizenship.

Notes

INCOME INEQUALITY

75. THE FACT OF THE MATTER IS THAT, OVER THE PAST 40 YEARS, WE HAVE WITNESSED AN ENORMOUS TRANSFER OF WEALTH FROM THE MIDDLE CLASS TO THE TOP 1%. IN OTHER WORDS, WE ARE WITNESSING THE ROBIN HOOD PRINCIPLE IN REVERSE. WE ARE TAKING FROM THE POOR AND WORKING FAMILIES OF AMERICA AND GIVING TO THE VERY RICH.

76. WE ARE IN A SITUATION WHERE WE HAVE NOT BEEN SINCE THE LATE 1920'S, BEFORE THE DEPRESSION, WHERE THE TOP 1% OWNS 38% OF THE FINANCIAL WEALTH OF AMERICA, WHILE THE BOTTOM 60% OWNS 2.3% OF THE

WEALTH IN AMERICA. THAT IS OBSCENE BEYOND BELIEF.

77. AT A TIME WHEN MANY AMERICAN WORKERS ARE WORRIED ABOUT THEIR ABILITY TO RETIRE WITH DIGNITY, I CANNOT SUPPORT AN OMNIBUS APPROPRIATIONS BILL THAT COULD ALTER 40 YEARS OF FEDERAL LAW AND SUBSTANTIALLY LOWER PENSIONS FOR MILLIONS OF WORKERS. WE HAVE GOT TO STOP THE WAR AGAINST WORKING FAMILIES.

78. A NATION WILL NOT SURVIVE MORALLY OR ECONOMICALLY WHEN SO FEW HAVE SO MUCH, WHILE SO MANY HAVE SO LITTLE.

79. MY DAD CAME TO THIS COUNTRY AT THE AGE OF SEVENTEEN WITHOUT ANY MONEY. MY MOTHER HAD DREAMS TO OWN A

HOME OF HER OWN, A SMALL HOME, RATHER THAN RENT. MY DAD WORKED ALL OF THE TIME BUT HE NEVER MADE A LOT OF MONEY, SO THERE WAS ALWAYS PRESSURE IN THE FAMILY AND CONSTANT BICKERING. WHEN YOU'RE A KID, YOU PICK UP ON THAT. WHEN YOU DON'T HAVE A LOT OF MONEY, YOUR FAMILY LIVES UNDER STRESS. THAT'S HAPPENING ALL OVER AMERICA TODAY, AND THAT'S A LESSON THAT I HAVE NEVER FORGOTTEN.

80. IT IS ABSURD THAT MILLIONS OF WORKERS MAKING AS LITTLE AS $455 A WEEK ARE CONSIDERED 'SUPERVISORS' AND GET NO OVERTIME PAY.

81. THE SAD REALITY OF TODAY'S AMERICA IS THAT, WHILE THE WEALTHIEST PEOPLE AND LARGEST

corporations are doing phenomenally well, the middle class is disappearing, and millions of Americans are working longer hours for lower wages. Congress must start listening to the needs of ordinary Americans, not just the billionaire class and their lobbyists...

82. There is far too little discussion [in Washington] about the collapse of the middle class... Almost no discussion at all about the incredible income and wealth inequality in this country and the fact that we're moving toward an oligarchic form of society.

83. There is a war going on in this country, and I am not

TALKING ABOUT THE WAR IN IRAQ OR THE WAR IN AFGHANISTAN. I AM TALKING ABOUT A WAR BEING WAGED BY SOME OF THE WEALTHIEST AND MOST POWERFUL PEOPLE IN THIS COUNTRY AGAINST THE WORKING FAMILIES OF THE UNITED STATES. AGAINST THE DISAPPEARING AND SHRINKING MIDDLE CLASS OF OUR COUNTRY. THE BILLIONAIRES OF AMERICA ARE ON THE WAR PATH. THEY WANT MORE, AND MORE, AND MORE.

84. WE HAVE A RIGGED ECONOMY, WHERE MOST NEW WEALTH FLOWS TO THE TOP 1%. THE SYSTEM IS HELD IN PLACE BY CORRUPT POLITICS WHERE WALL STREET BANKS AND BILLIONAIRES BUY ELECTIONS.

85. They talk about class warfare – the fact of the matter is there has been class warfare for the last thirty years. It's a handful of billionaires taking on the entire middle-class and working-class of this country. And the result is you now have in America the most unequal distribution of wealth and income of any major country on Earth and the worst inequality in America since 1928. How could anybody defend the top 400 richest people in this country owning more wealth than the bottom half of America, 150 million people?

86. Millions are unemployed and our roads and bridges are falling apart. If we can spend

6 TRILLION DOLLARS SENDING PEOPLE TO WAR, WE CAN SPEND 1 TRILLION TO PUT AMERICANS TO WORK FIXING OUR NATION'S CRUMBLING INFRASTRUCTURE. LET'S REBUILD AMERICA AND CREATE JOBS.

87. TODAY, THE UNITED STATES IS NUMBER ONE IN BILLIONAIRES, NUMBER ONE IN CORPORATE PROFITS, NUMBER ONE IN CEO SALARIES, NUMBER ONE IN CHILDHOOD POVERTY AND NUMBER ONE IN INCOME AND WEALTH INEQUALITY IN THE INDUSTRIALIZED WORLD.

88. THE RICH GET RICHER. EVERYONE ELSE GETS POORER. THE WEALTHIEST 8 AMERICANS INCREASED THEIR WEALTH BY MORE THAN $87 BILLION IN 2014. THAT'S MORE THAN OUR NATION

SPENDS ON FOOD STAMPS – WHICH REPUBLICANS WANT TO CUT.

89. EVERY CANDIDATE FOR PRESIDENT MUST ANSWER THE FOLLOWING QUESTIONS: IS IT MORALLY APPROPRIATE THAT 99% OF ALL NEW INCOME IS GOING TO THE TOP 1%? IS IT GOOD ECONOMICS THAT THE TOP ONE-TENTH OF 1% OWN ALMOST AS MUCH WEALTH AS THE BOTTOM 90%? IS OUR DEMOCRACY BEING DESTROYED WHEN ONE FAMILY CAN SPEND $900 MILLION TO BUY ELECTIONS?

Notes

MINIMUM WAGE

90. We must be talking about how we create the millions of jobs our economy desperately needs, how we address the crisis of low-wage to a living wage, among many other issues facing the disappearing middle class.

91. A job should lift workers out of poverty, not keep them in it.

92. Nobody who works 40 hours a week should be living in poverty.

93. Understand that Donald Trump thinks a low minimum wage in America is a good idea. He thinks low wages are a good idea.

94. The reality is that most of the new jobs being created in our economy today are low-wage and part-time jobs… What we need to do now is not only raise the minimum wage to give working people more disposable income, but we need to rebuild our infrastructure; we need to put real dollars in the hands of working people to improve their standard of living. And when you do that, they have the money to spend and create additional jobs.

95. At a time when the middle class is disappearing and millions of working Americans are still living in poverty, it is absolutely imperative that we raise the

MINIMUM WAGE. I AM VERY DISAPPOINTED, BUT NOT SURPRISED, THAT ONLY ONE REPUBLICAN AGREED TO EVEN CONSIDER THE LEGISLATION.

NOTES

SOCIAL SECURITY

96. Right now, billionaires pay in to the Social Security trust fund the same amount of money as someone making $110,000 a year. And if we lift that cap to $250,000, if you just do that, Social Security will be solvent for the next 75 years.

97. They told us that Social Security would go broke, that it could not possibly succeed. These critics were wrong 73 years ago, and they are wrong today.

Notes

TAXES

98. WHAT KIND OF NATION ARE WE WHEN WE GIVE TAX BREAKS TO BILLIONAIRES, BUT WE CAN'T TAKE CARE OF THE ELDERLY AND THE CHILDREN?

99. WANT TO BETTER UNDERSTAND WHY WE HAVE A FEDERAL DEFICIT? IN 1952, THE CORPORATE INCOME TAX ACCOUNTED FOR ABOUT 33% OF ALL FEDERAL TAX REVENUE. TODAY, DESPITE RECORD BREAKING PROFITS, CORPORATE TAXES BRING IN LESS THAN 9%. IT'S TIME FOR REAL TAX REFORM.

100. CORPORATIONS CAN'T HAVE IT BOTH WAYS. THEY CAN'T TELL AMERICANS HOW MUCH THEY WANT US TO BUY THEIR PRODUCTS, BUT THEN RUN ABROAD TO AVOID TAXES OR HIRE

cheap labor. American corporations should pay their fair share of taxes and create decent-paying jobs here – not in China.

101. We're going to do away with corporate loopholes that allow major profitable corporations to stash their money in the Cayman Islands and not pay a nickel in some cases, in federal income tax.

102. The United States is the only major country on Earth that does not in one form or another regulate prescription drug prices and the results have been an unmitigated disaster. In just the last two years, generic drug price increases cost American taxpayers an

ADDITIONAL SEVEN-HUNDRED MILLION DOLLARS.

103. INSTEAD OF TALKING ABOUT CUTS IN SOCIAL SECURITY, MEDICARE AND MEDICAID, WE MUST END THE ABSURDITY OF CORPORATIONS NOT PAYING A NICKEL IN FEDERAL INCOME TAXES.

104. THE NATIONAL DEBT WAS PRIMARILY CAUSED BY THE WAR IN IRAQ, HUGE TAX BREAKS FOR THE WEALTHY AND BIG CORPORATIONS, A PRESCRIPTION DRUG PROGRAM WRITTEN BY THE PHARMACEUTICAL INDUSTRY, AND THE DEREGULATION OF WALL STREET THAT PRECIPITATED THE WORST ECONOMIC RECESSION SINCE THE 1930'S.

105. The CEO of Goldman Sachs is telling the American people to lower their expectations for benefits from Social Security, Medicare and Medicaid so that he and his wealthy friends can keep their tax breaks. Just think about the arrogance of these guys on Wall Street who were bailed out by the middle class of this country when their greed nearly destroyed the international financial system and now they lecture the American people about the need to cut programs from working families who are struggling because of the recession they caused. Maybe the CEO's on Wall Street should lower their expectations before working folks lower theirs.

106. When you pay people at Walmart starvation wages and you don't provide benefits, who picks up the difference? The answer is that many of the workers in Walmart end up getting Medicaid; they get food stamps; they get affordable housing paid for by the taxpayers of this country – while the Walton family remains the wealthiest family in the country. If that is not obscene, I don't know what it.

107. It turns out that Walmart is the largest recipient of welfare in America.

108. This country does in fact have a serious deficit problem. But the reality is

that the deficit was caused by two wars – unpaid for. It was caused by huge tax breaks for the wealthiest people in this country. It was caused by a recession as a result of the greed, recklessness and illegal behavior on Wall Street. And if those are the causes of the deficit, I will be damned if we're going to balance the budget on backs of the elderly, the sick, the children, and the poor. That's wrong.

109. Want to know why we need real tax reform? Over the past six years, General Electric made nearly $34 billion in profits in the United States. What was their federal tax bill? Zero. No, less than zero. They received a tax rebate

FROM THE IRS OF NEARLY THREE BILLION, AFTER STASHING MUCH OF THEIR CASH IN THE BAHAMAS, BERMUDA AND OTHER OFFSHORE TAX HAVENS.

110. THE RICH PEOPLE APPARENTLY ARE LEAVING AMERICA. THEY'RE GIVING UP THEIR CITIZENSHIP. THESE GREAT LOVERS OF AMERICA WHO MADE THEIR MONEY IN THIS COUNTRY – WHEN YOU ASK THEM TO PAY THEIR FAIR SHARE OF TAXES, THEY'RE RUNNING ABROAD. WE HAVE 19 YEAR OLD KIDS WHO DIED IN IRAQ AND AFGHANISTAN DEFENDING THIS COUNTRY. THEY WENT ABROAD, NOT TO ESCAPE TAXES; THEY'RE WORKING CLASS KIDS WHO DIED IN WARS AND NOW THE BILLIONAIRES WANT TO RUN ABROAD TO AVOID PAYING THEIR FAIR SHARE OF TAXES.

What patriotism! What love of country!

111. Wall Street and the largest corporations in the country must begin to pay their fair share of taxes. They must not be able to continue hiding their profits offshore and shipping American jobs overseas to avoid taxes.

112. For too many years, we've underfunded our nation's physical infrastructure. We have to change that and that's what the Rebuild America Act is all about. We must modernize our infrastructure and create 13 million new jobs that will put people back to work and help the economy.

Notes

TRADE POLICY

113. WE MUST END OUR DISASTROUS TRADE POLICIES WHICH ENABLE CORPORATE AMERICA TO SHUT DOWN PLANTS IN THIS COUNTRY AND MOVE TO CHINA AND OTHER LOW-WAGE COUNTRIES.

NOTES

VALUES AND PRINCIPLES

114. Do you think it is moral that 20% of the children in this country are living in poverty?

115. It's not a radical concept that maybe the United States government should represent working families rather than a handful of billionaires.

116. Under normal times, it's fine if you have a moderate Democrat running, a moderate Republican running [for the presidency]. These are not normal times. The United States right now is in the

MIDDLE OF A SEVERE CRISIS AND YOU HAVE TO CALL IT WHAT IT IS.

117. WHEN BUSH WAS PRESIDENT, REPUBLICANS VOTED FOR FIVE EXTENSIONS OF EMERGENCY UNEMPLOYMENT WITHOUT ANY OFFSETS. THAT WAS WHEN BUSH WAS PRESIDENT. OBAMA IS PRESIDENT, IT BECOMES A DIFFERENT STORY.

118. ENOUGH IS ENOUGH. THIS GREAT NATION AND ITS GOVERNMENT BELONG TO ALL OF THE PEOPLE AND NOT TO A HANDFUL OF BILLIONAIRES, THEIR SUPER PACS AND THEIR LOBBYISTS.

119. IF YOU LOOK AT THE NEWSPAPERS HERE – THE WASHINGTON PAPERS – MOST OF THE DISCUSSION DEALS WITH CAMPAIGN GOSSIP.

120. This country is never going to move forward unless we end right-wing rule in the House.

121. The Republican debate is over, and not one word about economic inequality, climate change, Citizens United or student debt. And that's why the Republicans are so out of touch.

122. We are moving toward an oligarchic form of society, where the billionaires will control the economy and the political life of this country.

123. Billionaires are giving very strong support to elected officials who will do exactly the opposite of what the

American people want. I think that's a pretty pathetic situation. This is how corrupt Washington has become.

124. A few wealthy individuals and corporations have bought up our private sector and now they're buying up our government. We must overturn Citizens United and restore the power of the people.

125. We need a constitutional amendment to overturn Citizens United and, in fact, we need public funding of elections, so that all candidates have a fair shot at getting elected and they can be judged by their ideas, by what they're fighting for,

AND NOT BY THE BANK ACCOUNTS OF THEIR CAMPAIGN SPONSORS.

NOTES

VETERANS

126. The fact that on any given night there are fifty thousand homeless veterans on the street is a national disgrace.

127. How is it that we can afford to allow 1 in 4 major corporations to not pay federal taxes, but we can't afford to help our veterans?

128. Taking care of our veterans is a cost of war. If you can spend six trillion dollars sending people to war, you can spend a few billion dollars taking care of them when they come home.

129. If you are not prepared to take care of the men and

WOMEN WHO PUT THEIR LIVES ON THE LINE TO DEFEND THIS COUNTRY – WHO CAME BACK WOUNDED IN BODY, WOUNDED IN SPIRIT – IF YOU'RE NOT PREPARED TO HELP THOSE PEOPLE, THEN DON'T SEND THEM TO WAR IN THE FIRST PLACE.

Notes

WALL STREET

130. IF A BANK IS TOO BIG TO FAIL, IT'S TOO BIG TO EXIST.

131. THREE OF THE FOUR LARGEST FINANCIAL INSTITUTIONS ARE NEARLY 80% LARGER THAN THEY WERE WHEN WE BAILED THEM OUT.

132. IT IS NOT THE CONGRESS THAT REGULATES WALL STREET – IT'S WALL STREET THAT REGULATES THE US CONGRESS.

133. TEACHERS DID NOT CAUSE THIS RECESSION. FIREFIGHTERS AND POLICE OFFICERS… DID NOT CAUSE THIS RECESSION. THIS RECESSION WAS CAUSED BY THE GREED, THE RECKLESSNESS AND ILLEGAL BEHAVIOR OF THE PEOPLE ON WALL STREET.

134. It should make every American very nervous that in this weak regulatory environment, the financial supervisors in this country and around the world are still able to uncover an enormous amount of fraud on Wall Street to this day. I fear very much that the financial system is even more fragile than many people may perceive. This huge issue cannot be swept under the rug. It has got to be addressed.

135. Wall Street's economic and political power is a huge danger to the future of our country. As we have seen in the recent omnibus appropriations bill, it is not

Congress which regulates Wall Street but Wall Street which regulates Congress. The solution: The major Wall Street banks must be broken up, and I will introduce legislation to do that.

NOTES

WAR

136. TWO WARS ARE ENOUGH. LET'S COME HOME AND ADDRESS OUR SERIOUS PROBLEMS.

137. AFTER 14 YEARS IN AFGHANISTAN AND 12 YEARS IN IRAQ, AFTER THE LOSS OF ALMOST 7,000 TROOPS AND THE EXPENDITURE OF TRILLIONS OF DOLLARS, I VERY MUCH FEAR U.S. INVOLVEMENT IN AN EXPANDING AND NEVER-ENDING QUAGMIRE IN THAT REGION OF THE WORLD.

138. OUR FOREIGN POLICY HAS FAILED THE AMERICAN PEOPLE AND LED TO WARS LIKE THE WAR IN IRAQ WHICH WE SHOULD NEVER HAVE GOTTEN INTO.

139. REGIME CHANGE WITHOUT WORRYING ABOUT WHAT HAPPENS

THE DAY AFTER YOU GET RID OF THE DICTATOR DOES NOT MAKE A LOT OF SENSE. I HELPED LEAD THE EFFORT AGAINST THE WAR IN IRAQ. I ONLY WISH THAT I HAD BEEN SUCCESSFUL IN STOPPING THAT WAR GIVEN ALL THAT HAS HAPPENED SINCE; WITH THE RISE OF ISIS AND SO FORTH.

Notes

WOMEN'S RIGHTS

140. THE CURRENT ATTEMPT TO DISCREDIT PLANNED PARENTHOOD IS PART OF A LONG-TERM SMEAR CAMPAIGN BY PEOPLE WHO WANT TO DENY WOMEN IN THIS COUNTRY THE RIGHT TO CONTROL THEIR OWN BODIES.

141. THE RIGHT-WING IN THIS COUNTRY IS WAGING A WAR AGAINST WOMEN AND, LET ME BE VERY CLEAR, IT IS NOT A WAR THAT WE ARE GOING TO ALLOW THEM TO WIN.

142. THE DECISION ABOUT ABORTION MUST REMAIN A DECISION FOR A WOMAN AND HER DOCTOR TO MAKE, NOT THE GOVERNMENT.

Notes

Bernie Sanders

...

Quotes About Sanders
From His Supporters

Jon Stewart: "The problem isn't that Bernie Sanders is a crazy-pants cuckoo bird. It's that we've all become so accustomed to stage-managed, focus-group-driven candidates that his authenticity comes across as lunacy."

The Most Interesting Man in the World: "I don't always trust politicians, but when I do, it's Bernie Sanders."

John Fugelsang @JohnFugelsang (Twitter): "They tell me @SenSanders can't win b/c America won't vote for a Socialist Jew. I tell them America celebrates a Socialist Jew every Dec 25."

Ross Wheeler: "So amazing that Bernie is still standing by his beliefs he has held for so long, unlike some

WHO CHANGE DEPENDING ON POLITICAL CLIMATE."

<u>Anita Van Tubergen</u>: "Bernie, as a mother of a young daughter, my first priority is her. I believe that you will fight for the generations to come by helping combat climate change! For that reason and many others as well, you have my continued contributions and support!

<u>Robert Halenda</u>: "Bernie is not attempting to construct a socialist state. He is not trying to make people dependent on the government. He does not want to give people a bunch of 'free stuff.' The aim of Senator Sanders is to rebalance the priorities of the American government into a top-down system based on maximizing the standard of living. This is through reimplementing programs of the past (free university-level higher education, a living wage relevant to the inflation level) and taking ideas that work from other

nations (the health care systems of greater Europe and the social democratic models of Scandinavia in particular). If you choose to believe it is impossible to make an egalitarian-focused government work alongside capitalism, that's your fault for limiting your field of vision, but I for one have hope for a future."

Kyle Stark: "Bernie is the reason I am choosing to study Politics, Philosophy and Economics at university this year. I want to be a positive force in the world like this man. Change is needed and together we, the people, can bring it about."

Cheryl Wheeler: "Bernie gives me goosebumps when I listen to him! I remember before he was running I posted on [his Facebook page] 'Please run for president… you're our only hope.' … I meant it and I'm so proud of how far Bernie has come. I'm dumbfounded by the people who are so against what Bernie stands for.

THE CITIZENS OF THIS COUNTRY ARE SO DIVIDED I BELIEVE SOME OF MY FRIENDS WANT NOTHING TO DO WITH ME BECAUSE I STAND WITH BERNIE... IT'S JUST A FEELING I HAVE AND HONESTLY, I'D RATHER HAVE BERNIE AS PRESIDENT THEN TO KEEP THOSE FRIENDS ANYWAY... THIS ELECTION IS WAY TOO IMPORTANT! I ALSO TRULY BELIEVE THAT ALL THE BERNIE HATERS WHO KEEP CALLING HIM A COMMUNIST AND A SOCIALIST AND KEEP TALKING ABOUT HOW BERNIE IS GOING TO TAKE ALL THEIR MONEY JUST HAVE NO CLUE WHAT THEY ARE TALKING ABOUT AND ARE TOO STUBBORN TO REALLY READ UP ON BERNIE AND WHAT HE STANDS FOR. HE'S THE ONLY CANDIDATE WHO WILL BRING DEMOCRACY BACK... SOMETIMES I QUESTION MYSELF... 'AM I AN IDIOT FOR BELIEVING IN BERNIE?'... I COME TO MY SENSES AND REALIZE THEY ARE THE IDIOTS. GO BERNIE!"

RYAN MCDERMOTT: "ADVOCATING FOR BERNIE IS GREAT, BUT EVEN MORE IMPORTANT IS TO MAKE SURE YOU ARE REGISTERED TO VOTE AND VOTE IN THE PRIMARIES AND CAUCUSES TO ENSURE HE

BECOMES THE DEMOCRATIC NOMINATION."

ERIC PALI: "PRESIDENT THIS MAN ALREADY."

ZEYEAD HOSSAM GHARIB: "WATCH 'THE BIG SHORT' AND GET ANGRY. THIS IS WHAT BANKING IN AMERICA HAS BECOME. THEY NEED REGULATION. THEY NEED U.S. SENATOR BERNIE SANDERS. THE MOVIE'S DIRECTOR ALREADY ENDORSED HIM!"

WILL SPOJA: "I LIKE HOW RUBIO IS SO BUSY CAMPAIGNING THAT HE CAN'T BE BOTHERED TO VOTE ON ANYTHING; MEANWHILE BERNIE IS NOT ONLY VOTING, HE'S ACTUALLY INTRODUCING BILLS! THAT'S THE KIND OF WORK ETHIC WE NEED IN THE WHITE HOUSE."

SETH BENNY THOMAS: "BERNIE SANDERS SUPPORTERS; RESTORING MY FAITH IN HUMANITY ONE PERSON AT A TIME."

MAKADE NORTON: "LIVING IN A STATE WHERE MY VOTE BASICALLY DOESN'T COUNT DUE TO GERRYMANDERING AND STRONG REPUBLICAN VIEWS, I WILL SAY THAT I SUPPORT BERNIE SANDERS AS A

PRESIDENT. I'M NOT A CRAZY PERSON WHO THINKS I'M GOING TO BE RICH; MOST PEOPLE ARE JUST MIDDLE CLASS. I LIKE ALL THAT BERNIE STANDS FOR! THE MILLENNIALS CAN HELP HIM WIN THIS!"

<u>JON MCFARLAND</u>: "THANK YOU BERNIE FOR RESTORING MY FAITH IN OUR NATION'S POLITICAL PROCESS. JUST DONATED 10$ THE OTHER DAY AND WILL SOON BE DONATING MY FIRST EVER PRESIDENTIAL VOTE FOR YOU IN THE UPCOMING YEAR!"

<u>MIKE WRIGHT</u>: "HONESTY AND INTEGRITY. A MAN WHO WILL RESTORE THE ECONOMIC FUTURE FOR ALL AMERICANS. BERNIE SANDERS IS THAT MAN. SANDERS SAVES 2016."

<u>MAUREEN VICTORIA</u>: "I AM 62, WORK FT AT A STRESSFUL JOB THAT PAYS LESS THAN IT DID 25 YEARS AGO, AND HAVE MULTIPLE HEALTH PROBLEMS THAT MY EMPLOYER PUNISHES ME FURTHER FOR. SENATOR SANDERS IS MY ONLY HOPE FOR ANY SORT OF DECENT RETIREMENT. I LOST ALL MY SAVINGS, MY HOME, MY CREDIT STANDING SINCE THE BANKING SYSTEM'S COLLAPSE IN 2008."

LORRAINE VIGORITI: "This is an election for the future of this nation. It's more about the long term effects that our next president will inspire in our citizens. If we do not elect Bernie, then I fear that all will be lost... Consider the children carefully when casting your vote..."

SHARON HALL ESKEW: "The truth shall be told by the only candidate I will vote for...Bernie Sanders needs to be the next President of the United States! Bernie or Bust!"

BRENDAN FINCH: "Bernie Sanders is the revolution. Fight class war. Bern em Bernie."

ROBERT PHILLIPS: "Bernie Sanders isn't bullshitting anyone. He stands for major change in a fraud-ridden, completely rigged economy. The average American, I am sad to say, has an understanding of issues equal to a six year old, and haven't ever stopped to think for themselves about much of anything.

BUT I SENSE THAT BERNIE'S GRASSROOTS SUPPORT IS EVEN STRONGER THAN IT APPEARS, BECAUSE THERE ARE STILL ENOUGH AMERICANS WHO DO CARE, AND WHO DO UNDERSTAND THAT HE IS THE ONLY CANDIDATE WHO REPRESENTS THEIR INTERESTS."

<u>Mark Melia</u>: "Thanks Sen. Sanders! This veteran is voting Bernie in 2016!"

<u>Linda Parena</u>: "Bernie is right on about every issue."

<u>Barbara A. Manginelli</u>: "Bernie Sanders. A man with ideas whose time has come!"

<u>Mary Mullins</u>: "President Bernie Sanders 2016! The ONLY candidate who is NOT FOR SALE! VOTE!"

Notable Endorsements

As of December 2015

Celebrities

Kareem Abdul-Jabbar, NBA Hall of Fame inductee and author
Courtney Act, drag performer, television personality, and singer
Ted Alexandro, stand-up comedian
All Shall Perish, deathcore band
Joanna Angel, director, writer, and actress of adult films
Richmond Arquette, actor
Bun B, rapper
Brian Baker, former guitarist for Bad Religion and Minor Threat
Chris Ballew, lead singer of The Presidents of the United States of America
Lou Barlow, musician and songwriter for Dinosaur Jr. and Sebadoh
Roseanne Barr, actress, comedian, producer, and writer
Justin Bartha, actor

- Gerry Beckley, singer-songwriter and musician for America
- Michael Bennett, NFL football player for the Seattle Seahawks.
- Bhi Bhiman, singer-songwriter
- Jello Biafra, former singer for the Dead Kennedys
- Big Boi, rapper, songwriter, and member of Outkast
- Stephen Bishop, actor
- Elvin Bishop, blues and rock musician
- Cedric Bixler-Zavala, musician
- Lewis Black, comedian
- Michael Ian Black, comedian, actor, and writer
- Billy Bragg, musician
- Olga Breeskin, violinist, dancer, and actress
- Madeline Brewer, actress
- Nicholas Britell, composer, pianist, and film producer
- Mehcad Brooks, actor
- Jackson Browne, singer-songwriter
- Dewey Bunnell, singer-songwriter and guitarist for America
- Butterscotch, singer and beatboxer
- Dan Campbell, lead vocalist of The Wonder Years

Richard Campbell, musician, singer-songwriter, and record producer
Belinda Carlisle, lead singer of the The Go-Go's
Julian Casablancas, singer-songwriter and lead singer of The Strokes
Tommy Castro, singer-songwriter and musician
Reg E. Cathey, actor
Matthew Caws, lead of Nada Surf, songwriter, and guitarist
Chapin Sisters, folk rock duo: Abigail and Lily Chapin
Margaret Cho, comedian and actress
Tommy Chong, comedian, actor, and activist
Best Coast, two-piece rock band: Bethany Cosentino and Bobb Bruno
Frankie Cosmos, singer-songwriter and musician
Daniel Craig, actor
Marshall Crenshaw, singer-songwriter and musician
David Crosby, singer-songwriter and musician
John Cusack, actor
Bob D'Amico, drummer for The Fiery Furnaces and Sebadoh

- William Daniels, actor and former member of the Screen Actors Guild
- William B. Davis, actor and environmental activist
- Dead Heavens, blues rock band
- John Densmore, drummer of the The Doors, writer, and actor
- Kevin Devine, singer-songwriter and musician
- Danny DeVito, actor, producer, and director
- Ani DiFranco, singer, guitarist, poet and songwriter
- Diplo, DJ, songwriter, and producer
- Jimmy Dore, comedian and host of The Jimmy Dore Show
- David Draiman, lead singer for Disturbed
- Joe Driscoll, multi-instrumentalist, rapper, and beatboxer
- Greg Dulli, singer for Afghan Whigs
- Eliza Dushku, actress
- Steve Earle, rock, singer-songwriter, record producer, author and actor
- Alex Ebert, Ima Robot and Edward Sharpe and the Magnetic Zeros lead singer

EL-P, musician, entrepreneur, and half of Run the Jewels

Alejandro Escovedo, singer-songwriter

Mia Farrow, actress, activist, and former fashion model

FDA Music, rapper

Will Ferrell, actor and comedian

Frances Fisher, actress

Jon Fishman, drummer and co-founder of Phish

Jon Fitch, mixed martial artist

Flea, bassist for the Red Hot Chili Peppers

Ben Foster, actor

Jon Foster, actor and musician

Mark Foster, musician and lead singer for Foster the People

Kinky Friedman, singer-songwriter, novelist, humorist, and politician

Bill Frisell, guitarist and composer

Gang Gang Dance, experimental band

G-Eazy, rapper and producer

Nicholas Gonzalez, actor

Mike Gordon, bass-guitar and vocals for Phish

Billy Gould, producer and bassist for Faith No More.

Kristen Gundred, singer-songwriter and founder of Dum Dum Girls
Deidre Hall, actress and activist
Halsey, singer/songwriter and recording artist
Brian Hamilton, actor and voice actor
Kay Hanley, musician and former singer for Letters to Cleo
Daryl Hannah, actress and activist
Maureen Herman, writer and bass player for Babes in Toyland
Torri Higginson, actress
Brendan Hines, actor and musician
David Holden, screenwriter
Jana Hunter, lead singer for Lower Dens
Scott Ian, singer-songwriter and musician for Anthrax
Vincent Kartheiser, actor
Mimi Kennedy, actress and activist
Anthony Kiedis, singer for the Red Hot Chili Peppers
Laura Kightlinger, actress, comedian, and writer
Killer Mike, activist, musician, and half of Run the Jewels
Nate Kinsella, musician, member of Joan of Arc and Make Believe

Tim Kinsella, musician, member of Joan of Arc, Owls, and Make Believe
Josh Klinghoffer, guitarist for the Red Hot Chili Peppers
David Koechner, character actor and comedian
Wayne Kramer, guitarist for the MC5
Zoe Kravitz, actress, singer, and model
Rachelle Lefevre, actress and activist
Donovan Leitch, actor
Juliette Lewis, actress and singer
Lil B, rapper and producer
Jason Loewenstein, singer-songwriter and musician for The Fiery Furnaces and Sebadoh
Justin Long, actor
George Lopez, actor and comedian
Seth MacFarlane, creator of Family Guy, American Dad!, and The Cleveland Show
Jesse Malin, singer-songwriter and musician
Sal Masekela, actor, singer, and television personality
Dave Matthews, singer-songwriter and guitarist for Dave Matthews Band
Holt McCallany, actor, writer, and producer

- Cass McCombs, singer-songwriter and musician
- Justin Meldal-Johnsen, musician and songwriter
- Breckin Meyer, actor and musician
- Alyssa Milano, actress, singer, and producer
- Ezra Miller, actor
- Ryan Miller, lead singer and guitarist for Guster
- Hasan Minhaj, actor, comedian, and correspondent on The Daily Show
- Anaïs Mitchell, singer-songwriter and musician
- D.W. Moffett, actor
- Alfred Molina, actor
- Thurston Moore, singer and guitarist for Sonic Youth
- Viggo Mortensen, actor, writer, poet, artist, and musician
- Charlie Musselwhite, musician and bandleader
- Graham Nash, singer-songwriter and musician
- Meshell Ndegeocello, singer-songwriter, musician, and rapper
- Alexis Nelson, singer-songwriter, guitarist and activist

Will Noon, former drummer for Straylight Run
Tyler Oakley, media personality, humorist, and author
Patton Oswalt, comedian, writer, and actor
Amanda Palmer, singer-songwriter, musician, half of The Dresden Dolls and Evelyn Evelyn
Holly Palmer, singer-songwriter
Pants Velour, hip hop group
Rhea Perlman, actress
Jeremy Piven, actor and producer
Shira Piven, actress, producer, and movie director
Joel Rafael, singer-songwriter and folk musician
Bonnie Raitt, singer-songwriter, musician, and activist
Emily Ratajkowski, model and actress
Nathaniel Rateliff, singer-songwriter
Nikki Reed, actress, screenwriter, and singer-songwriter
John C. Reilly, actor, singer, and writer
Carl Reiner, actor, director, producer, and writer
Duke Robillard, musician

Joe Rogan, stand-up comedian and actor
Henry Rollins, musician, writer, actor, and activist
Tim Roth, actor and director
Ronda Rousey, UFC fighter
Mark Ruffalo, actor, director, producer, and screenwriter
Matthew Ryan, singer-songwriter and musician
Jonathan Sadowski, actor
Gabe Saporta, lead singer of Cobra Starship
Susan Sarandon, actress and activist
Scarface, rapper, music producer, and author
Chris Schlarb, musician, composer, and producer
Walter Schreifels, musician and producer
Reid Scott, actor
Peggy Seeger, singer and musician
Will Sheff, lead singer for Okkervil River
Chris Shiflett, guitarist for Foo Fighters, No Use for a Name, and Me First and the Gimme Gimmes
Corky Siegel, musician, singer-songwriter, and composer

Wanderlei Silva, retired UFC fighter and former Pride FC champion.
Sarah Silverman, stand-up comedian, writer, producer, and actress
Chad Smith, drummer for the Red Hot Chili Peppers
Bill Smitrovich, actor
Jill Sobule, musician
Sam Sparro, singer-songwriter and producer
Spirit Family Reunion, folk band
Spose, rapper and producer
Cole Sprouse, actor
Tommie Sunshine, record producer, songwriter, and DJ
Serj Tankian, singer for System of a Down
Corey Taylor, singer-songwriter and musician for Slipknot and Stone Sour
Donnette Thayer, singer-songwriter and guitarist for Game Theory and Hex
Tennessee Thomas, musician and actress
Maura Tierney, actress
Fat Tony, rapper

Jeff Tweedy, songwriter, musician, producer, and lead singer for Wilco
Dick Van Dyke, actor, comedian, and producer
Milana Vayntrub, actress, comedian, writer, and producer
Loudon Wainwright III, singer-songwriter and actor
Roger Waters, musician and co-founder of Pink Floyd
Mike Watt, musician and co-founder of Minutemen, Dos, and Firehose
Reggie Watts, musician, singer, beatboxer, actor, and comedian
Dusty Watson, drummer, most notably for The Sonics
George Wendt, actor
Wil Wheaton, actor and writer
Lucinda Williams, singer-songwriter
Saul Williams, rapper, actor, and activist
Lizz Winstead, comedian, media personality, and co-creator of The Daily Show
Yoni Wolf, musician and co-founder of Anticon
Neil Young, singer-songwriter and musician

Mas Ysa, musician, composer, and visual artist
Yung Skeeter, DJ and producer
Hans Zimmer, composer and producer
Z-Trip, DJ and producer
Sasheer Zamata, actress and comedian
Buckwheat Zydeco, musician
Newspapers and other media
Addison County Independent, Middlebury, Vermont
Ring of Fire, radio program

Journalists and Commentators

Brent Budowsky, journalist
Dan Carlin, historian, journalist, and host of Common Sense and Hardcore History
Alan Colmes, host of The Alan Colmes Show, former co-host of Hannity and Colmes, political commentator for Fox News Channel and blogger
Liza Featherstone, journalist and author
John Fugelsang, comedian, actor, and host of Tell Me Everything
Thom Hartmann, host of The Thom Hartmann Program and The Big Picture with Thom Hartmann

Doug Henwood, journalist and editor of Left Business Observer

John Iadarola, creator of ThinkTank

Ana Kasparian, co-host and producer of The Young Turks

Robert F. Kennedy Jr., environmentalist and co-host of Ring of Fire

Jamie Kilstein, writer, political comic, and host of Citizen Radio

Bill Maher, host of Real Time with Bill Maher

Mike Malloy, host of The Mike Malloy Show

Bill Moyers, journalist and former White House Press Secretary

John Nichols, journalist

David Pakman, host of The David Pakman Show

Mike Papantonio, attorney and co-host of Ring of Fire

Ron Reagan, journalist, former host of The Ron Reagan Show and Connected: Coast to Coast, and son of Ronald Reagan

Sam Seder, comedian, actor, and co-host of Ring of Fire

David Shuster, journalist

Ed Schultz, former host of The Ed Show and The Ed Schultz Show

Matt Taibbi, journalist
Jonathan Tasini, strategist, organizer, activist, and writer
Cenk Uygur, activist, co-founder of The Young Turks, and founder of Wolf PAC

Leaders in business

Ben Cohen, co-founder of Ben & Jerry's
Kim Dotcom, entrepreneur and political activist
Jerry Greenfield, co-founder of Ben & Jerry's
Howie Klein, writer, record label founder/executive, and political activist
Bhaskar Sunkara, founder of Jacobin Magazine
Steve Wozniak, co-founder of Apple Inc.

Scholars and critics

Linda Martín Alcoff, philosopher and activist
Dean Baker, Center for Economic and Policy Research co-founder

Wendy Brown, political scientist, author, and activist
Judy Cain – philosopher, mentor, activist and proffessor
Noam Chomsky, linguist, philosopher, and activist
Anthony Fantano, music blogger/vlogger behind The Needle Drop
Leon Fink, historian
Nancy Fraser, critical theorist and author
Jeffrey Guterman, psychologist
Steven Hahn, social and political historian
Gerald S. Handel, sociologist
Michael Hardt, philosopher and literary theorist
Carl Hart, psychologist
James M. Jasper, sociologist
Barbara Katz Rothman, sociologist
Stephanie Kelton, economist
David Korten, business scholar
Robert W. McChesney, media scholar
Walter Benn Michaels, literary theorist
Ruth Milkman, sociologist
Anne Norton, political scientist

Frances Fox Piven, sociologist and activist

Adolph L. Reed, Jr., political scientist and activist

Joel Selvin, music critic

Sylvie Simmons, rock historian

Rogers Smith, political scientist and author

Lester Spence, political scientist and social commentator

Zephyr Teachout, legal scholar and CEO of Mayday PAC

Cornel West, philosopher and activist

Jeffrey A. Winters, political scientist

Writers, filmmakers, and visual artists

Pat Bagley, editorial cartoonist

Sarah Childers, Writer and illustrator

Frank Darabont, screenwriter, film director and producer

Emek, designer, illustrator, and fine art painter

Lydia Emily, street artist, muralist, and oil painter

Ron English, contemporary artist

- Shepard Fairey, contemporary street artist, activist, and founder of OBEY
- Chris Gardner, screenwriter, film director, actor, producer and activist
- Sarah Hollister, writer, novelist, illustrator and activist
- Daniel Kellison, television and film producer
- Krystine Kryttre, alternative comics artist
- Spencer Madsen, contemporary writer and founding editor of Sorry House
- Adam McKay, screenwriter, director, comedian, and actor
- Michael Moore, documentary filmmaker and activist
- Brad Neely, comic book artist and television writer
- Annabel Park, documentary filmmaker and activist
- Oren Peli, director, producer, and screenwriter
- Anne Rice, novelist
- Sarah Della Town, writer and illustrator

Haskell Wexler, cinematographer, film producer and director

Labor Organizations - National

APWU - American Postal Workers Union, representing 250,000
CWA - Communication Workers of America, representing 700,000
NNU - National Nurses United, representing 185,000
NUHW - National Union of Healthcare Workers, representing 11,000
UE - United Electrical, Radio and Machine Workers of America, representing 35,900

Labor Organizations - State, Regional, and Local Divisions

AFL-CIO - American Federation of Labor and Congress of Industrial Organizations: VT, SC
IAIW - International Association of Bridge, Structural, Ornamental and

Reinforcing Iron Workers: Local 7 (MA)

IBEW - International Brotherhood of Electrical Workers: Locals 2222, 2313, 2321, 2322, 2323, 2324, 2325, 159, 440, 490 and 1837 (MA, RI, CA, ME, NH, WI)

ILWU - International Longshore and Warehouse Union: Inlandboatmen's Union of the Pacific

NEA - National Education Association: VT

SEIU - Service Employees International Union: Locals 560 and 1984 (NH)

Organizations

Democracy for America, advocacy group and PAC

Democratic Socialists of America, member of the Socialist International

Friends of the Earth, environmentalist group

Justice Party

Progressive Democrats of America, advocacy group and PAC

Social Democrats, USA, lapsed member of the Socialist International

Socialist Alternative, political party and member of the Committee for a Workers' International
USAction, NY Chapter
Vermont Progressive Party
Working Families Party

Activists, humanitarians, and labor leaders

Patch Adams, physician, comedian, social activist, clown, and author
Charles R. Chamberlain, Democracy for America Executive Director
Wade Davis, activist and former American football player
Jodie Evans, co-founder of CODEPINK
Bill McKibben, founder of climate change group 350.org
David McReynolds, former Socialist Party USA presidential nominee and former chair of the War Resisters League
Bruce Perens, free software advocate
Sal Rosselli, National Union of Healthcare Workers President
Yosi Sergant, publicist of the Barack Obama "Hope" poster

STANLEY SHEINBAUM, PEACE AND HUMAN RIGHTS ACTIVIST
DANIEL SIERADSKI, WRITER AND OCCUPY ACTIVIST
RICHARD STALLMAN, FOUNDER OF THE GNU PROJECT AND THE FREE SOFTWARE FOUNDATION
MARIANNE WILLIAMSON, FOUNDER OF PROJECT ANGEL FOOD
RAND WILSON, LABOR ACTIVIST

DEMOCRATIC PARTY FIGURES

TAD DEVINE, POLITICAL CONSULTANT
GARY KROEGER, 2016 U.S. HOUSE CANDIDATE (IA) AND ACTOR

STATE GOVERNORS - FORMER

JESSE VENTURA, 38TH GOVERNOR OF MINNESOTA (1999–2003) FOR THE REFORM PARTY

U.S. REPRESENTATIVES - CURRENT

KEITH ELLISON, MN
RAÚL GRIJALVA, AZ

State executive officials – Current

Doug Hoffer, Vermont Auditor of Accounts

State executive officials – Former

Dudley Dudley, New Hampshire Executive Council member (1977–1985)
Jim Hightower, Texas Agriculture Commissioner (1983–1991)
John Shea, New Hampshire Executive Council member (2006–2010)

State legislators - Current

Terry Alexander, SC Rep.
Tim Ashe, VT Sen. (VPP)
Jane Beaulieu, NH Rep.
Travis Bennett, NH Rep.
Steven Berry, VT Rep.
Peter Bixby, NH Rep.
Mollie Burke, VT Rep. (VPP)

Wayne Burton, NH Rep.
Mark Cardenas, AZ Rep.
Karen Clark, MN Rep.
Robin Chestnut-Tangerman, VT Rep. (VPP)
Renny Cushing, NH Rep.
Susan Davis, VT Rep. (VPP)
Gail Finney, KS Rep.
William Frank, VT Rep.
Patsy French, VT Rep.
Diana Gonzalez, VT Rep. (VPP)
Wendell Gilliard SC Rep.
Sandy Haas, VT Rep. (VPP)
Helen Head, VT Rep.
Geoffrey Hirsch, NH Rep.
Mary S. Hooper, VT Rep.
Marty Jack, NH Rep.
Troy Jackson, ME Sen.
Pramila Jayapal, WA Sen.
Warren Kitzmiller, VT Rep.
Patrick Long, NH Rep.
Linda Martin, VT Rep.
James McCullough, VT Rep.
Richard McNamara, NH Rep.
Juan Mendez, AZ Rep.
Marcia Moody, NH Rep.
Luis Moscoso, WA Rep.
Jean O'Sullivan, VT Rep.
Lee Oxenham, NH Rep.

Avram Patt, VT Rep.
Chris Pearson, VT Rep. (VPP)
Charles F. Pelkey, WY Rep.
Bill Perkins, NY Sen.
Anthony Pollina, VT Sen. (VPP)
Martín Quezada, AZ Sen.
Russell Ruderman, HI Sen.
Marjorie Ryerson, VT Rep.
James Sanders, Jr., NY Sen.
Andy Schmidt, NH Rep.
Tick Segerblom, NV Sen.
David Sharpe, VT Rep.
Gilman Shattuck, NH Rep.
Amy Sheldon, VT Rep.
Michael J. Skindell, OH Sen.
Timothy Smith, NH Rep.
Thomas Stevens, VT Rep.
Mary Sullivan, VT Rep.
George Sykes, NH Rep.
Robert Theberge, NH Rep.
Maida Townsend, VT Rep.
Joseph "Chip" Troiano, VT Rep.
Andy White, NH Rep.
Robert Q. Williams, SC Rep.
John Wisniewski, NJ Rep.
Mark Woodward, VT Rep.
Michael Yantachka, VT Rep.
Teo Žagar, VT Rep.
Will Guzzardi, IL Rep.

David Zuckerman, VT Sen. (VPP)

State legislators - Former

Mo Baxley, NH Rep. (2007–2008)
Daryl Beall, IA Sen. (2003–2014)
Gloria Bromell Tinubu, GA Rep. (2011)
Burt Cohen, NH Sen. (1990–2004)
Amanda Curtis, MT Rep. (2013–2015)
Thomas Duane, NY Sen. (1999–2012)
Matt Dunne, VT Sen. (2002–2006)
Eileen Ehlers, NH Rep. (2007–2008)
Tom Fiegen, IA Rep. (2000–2003)
Michael Foley, OH Rep. (2006–2014)
Sylvia Gale, NH Rep. (2012–2014)
Bev Hannon, IA Sen. (1985–1992)
Tom Hayden, CA Sen. (1992–2000)
Bob Perry, NH Rep. (2011–2014)
C. J. Prentiss, OH Sen. (1999–2006)
Nina Turner, OH Sen. (2008–2014)
Tom Turnipseed, SC Sen. (1976–1980)
Brian Wazlaw, NH Rep. (2012–2014)
Chuck Weed, NH Rep. (2000–2014)
John Wittneben, IA Rep. (2011–2013)

Mayors - Current

Daryl Justin Finizio, Mayor of New London, Connecticut

Mayors - Former

Rocky Anderson, 33rd Mayor of Salt Lake City (2000–2008); founder of the American Justice Party

Municipal Officials - Current

Rafael Espinal, New York City Councilor
Jesus "Chuy" Garcia, Cook County, IL Commissioner
Kshama Sawant, Seattle City Councilor

Municipal Officials - Former

Tim Hagan, Cuyahoga County, OH Commissioner (1982–1998, 2004–2011)

DNC Members - Current

Erin Bilbray, NV

Bernie Sanders

Richard Cassidy, VT
Larry Cohen, DC/CWA
Chad Nodland, ND

<u>DNC Members - Former</u>

Bill Press, former CA Dem. Party Chair

The Little Black Book

Bernie Sanders

The Little Black Book: 2016 Presidential Race series:

Hillary Clinton
Ted Cruz
Bernie Sanders
Donald Trump

More Titles in *The Little Black Book* series:

Albert Einstein
Aristotle
Benjamin Franklin
Bill Gates
Bruce Lee
Dale Carnegie
David Bowie
Elon Musk
Helen Keller
Johnny Depp
Justin Bieber
Mahatma Gandhi
Mark Twain
Martin Luther King Junior
Oprah Winfrey
Ralph Waldo Emerson
Richard Branson
Socrates
Stephen Hawking
Steve Jobs

If there is someone you'd like to see added to The Little Black Book series, you can contact Hollister on Facebook at www.facebook.com/SCHollister or contact us at www.RedPocketBookPublishing.com.

Bernie Sanders

Made in the USA
Middletown, DE
28 January 2016